Ants!
One, Three

Written by Pat O'Keefe
Illustrated by Sam Ward

Scott Foresman

The ants go in,

one by one.

How did the little one

get a bun?

The ants go in,

two by two.

Where did the little

one get a shoe?

The ants go in,

three by three.

Where did the little one

find a bee?

What do ants like to do?
Ants have fun.
We can have fun too!